ALL OUR HAPPY DAYS ARE STUPID

McSWEENEY'S
SAN FRANCISCO

ISBN 978-1-940450-79-7

www.mcsweeneys.net

COVER: Sara Cwynar, *Contemporary Floral Arrangement 3
(Flowers Arrangements 12,683 (1963))*, 2013,
Chromogenic print, 60 × 44 in., 152.4 × 111.76 cm.

ALL OUR
HAPPY DAYS
ARE STUPID

by Sheila Heti
with songs by Dan Bejar

by Sheila Heti

I wrote this play in 2001 for a feminist theatre company that never ended up staging it. They tried for years to make it into something of which any of us might have been proud, and in 2006, finally suggested that the play could run as a small production in an upcoming new-play festival. But after years of dramaturgical efforts to "improve" it, I had lost faith in the script and felt utterly confused by what it was, and said no. In the six years that followed, I felt like a failure and a quitter.

After abandoning the play, I began working in a more concentrated way on what became my novel, *How Should a Person Be?*, which began to incorporate the story of a Sheila who had been commissioned to write a play for a feminist theatre company, and failed. At various points during the writing of the book, I would put scenes from *All Our Happy Days Are Stupid* into it, then take them out, then put them back in, at one point thinking the whole second act of the book should be the second act of the play. My novel contained conversations between me and my friend Margaux Williamson; why not transition to another female friendship, also in dialogue, this one fictional—the friendship of Ms. Oddi and Mrs. Sing? Although this never worked, the play informed the book hugely. I published the novel in Canada in 2010.

A year later, the very talented writer and director Jordan Tannahill—whom I knew only passingly—contacted me after reading *How Should a Person Be?* to see if the play was real. After I sent him the script, he said he wanted to help me find a director for it. Then he said he would direct it himself. I was happy, skeptical, and afraid, since those frustrating years with the play were not far from memory, including my impatience with the actors' questions. Jordan's idea was to cast mostly non-actors—friends of his and mine—who might naturally understand the play and not ask method-y questions about their motivation, when the characters were never meant to be realistic in that way. He arranged for a backyard reading one summer afternoon so we could hear it. That afternoon, sitting around the table in the grass, for the first time ever the play felt like something real—quick and funny and better than I ever hoped it could be, no longer some ridiculous clanging thing. Also, everyone seemed to be having fun.

Jordan and his collaborator Erin Brubacher staged the play one year later, before a tiny audience of thirty-some people each night, who sat three feet from the narrow stage in two tight rows. Those nights of performances were the happiest weeks of my year, and gave me a dizzying feeling for how things go in life, sometimes. It took me writing the play, trying to improve it over the course of four years, giving up, feeling like a failure, writing about the failure in a book of fiction, then for the book to be a success, then for a man who was thirteen when the play was written to read this book and inquire about the script, for it to come to life.

Months after this production, on a cold, drunken evening in New York, Jordan Bass and Andrew Leland, two McSweeney's men from San Francisco, plus a bunch of mutual friends and my brother and I, were out at various bars late at night, when it was decided that it would be a really good idea for them to try their hand at theatre producing and bring the show to New York. Of course, it had to be McSweeney's—the name of a central character is Ms. Oddi, taken from the name of McSweeney's original printing house, Oddi Printing, based in Iceland, whom I was communicating with in late 2001 when I wrote the play, while simultaneously going through proofs for my first book, *The Middle Stories*, which McSweeney's published in the U.S. the following year.

Maybe everything comes to pass in convoluted ways, but it's only the most obviously convoluted events that make us see that this is so. We want things to proceed as we think they should, as would be most convenient to us—efficiently—or to happen in ways that fit our ideas of how things proceed for other people. Maybe our visions of perfection are optimistically happy, yet simple and basic and a little dumb. Because the commission didn't proceed as I felt it should, it was a bad day for me—a decade of bad days as far as my relationship to the play was concerned. But what ended up happening was far more interesting than anything I could have arranged in my head. Perhaps our vision of how life should be is actually no fun at all, and neglects to include the exciting people we have yet to meet, who make the stupid ways life seems to happen, happy after all.

by Jordan Tannahill

Why play?
 It's sort of the same question as "Why make a play?"

It's so easy to lose the thread of this question.

After years of workshops and feedback and rewrites and letdowns, what began as a play can feel like the furthest thing from playing. It becomes drudgery. It becomes a vortex of existential malaise and self-doubt. The imperfections and incongruities in our narratives and characters, the ones that first made them intriguing to us, are recast as problems to be fixed. But they cannot be fixed, not without killing the very essence of why we fell in love with the work in the first place. And sometimes, that's what we do—we kill a play. We kill characters, we kill subplots, we kill lines and scenes and jokes and images and ideas until there isn't a drop of blood or breath left.

When I asked Sheila if I could read *All Our Happy Days Are Stupid*, I asked her if I could read her original draft. The draft closest to her original impulses—the one that came before the countless revisions it was subjected to in its decade of dramaturgical purgatory. When I read that draft, I couldn't believe how much life there was in it. It was almost terrifyingly full of life. Sprawling, disorienting, profoundly insightful, and achingly funny, it was an unbridled and joyfully theatrical plunge into a truly Heti-esque universe.

I read the play in the summer of 2011, at a cottage. The man who owned this cottage had the head of a black bear mounted on his wall. I asked the man: Why would you kill and stuff a bear? He said, "Because he is sublime."

Because he is sublime. The only way he knew how to be with something so powerful and overwhelming was to kill and stuff it. His answer confounded and infuriated me. But then I realized that this is what had happened (or almost happened) to Sheila's play. Sometimes theatres are confronted with plays that are so overwhelming, they're at a loss as to how to "tackle" them—so they attempt to kill and stuff them instead. To neutralize their danger by removing their essence.

So how could I capture the beauty and power of Sheila's play without turning it into theatrical taxidermy? I had to return to the essential question: Why play? Why make a play? There was something so intuitive about asking a group of our friends to come together and give life to this. That was, after all, the only way I have ever known how to make theatre. It's also the most genuine answer I have to the "why play" question—the opportunity for friends to gather together to hear each other say strange and beautiful words. It's a way for us to become other people and, in so doing, to understand new facets of ourselves.

That summer Sheila and I organized a reading of the play in our friend Marc's backyard. We gathered together an eclectic group of mostly non-actors—a few artists, a few writers, a heart surgeon. And the bear of this play came to life. The things that never quite seemed to work before suddenly began to work. The group seemed to innately understand both the dry, offbeat humor and the quiet pathos that suffuses the piece. Something was unlocked by liberating the script from the standard strictures of development and production. And aesthetically, something resonated with our embrace of the amateur. Of the imperfect and incongruous.

Not long after that, we decided to do the show.

Erin Brubacher and I directed and produced the premiere at Videofag, a tiny storefront theatre I run with William Ellis in Toronto's Kensington Market neighborhood. We staged the show in a room measuring a little less than thirty feet by eleven feet, for an audience of thirty-three people—thirty-five, if two people sat on the speakers. It was a hurricane in a teacup, and never much felt like a night out at the theatre. More like a fabulous, surreal party that also happened to be a play. It reminded me how important it is to approach a play on its own terms. To change the context to suit a play, rather than changing the play to suit a context (e.g., a theatre).

"Why make a play?" has become particularly resonant for me with this production, particularly considering that most of the people onstage are not formally trained, professional actors. Why come together and do this ridiculous and vulnerable thing night after night? When I watch *All Our Happy Days Are Stupid*, I am always aware of the meta-narrative at work: the story of friends coming together to put on a show that no one else would. And most importantly, the story of a group of people who have attempted, since embarking on this adventure, to never lose sight of the pleasure of playing.

Characters

JENNY ODDI	A twelve-year-old girl, young for her age
MS. ODDI	Jenny's mother, vain and a little glamorous
MR. ODDI	Jenny's father, not very masculine, kind
DANIEL SING	A twelve-year-old boy, an individual
MRS. SING	Daniel's mother, tense and hostile
MR. SING	Daniel's father, silent and strong
DAN	Daniel, thirties, a famous singer and recluse; the singer
PLURABELLE	Owns the Paris hotel, an older woman, grey-haired
THE HANDSOME MAN WHO DOESN'T KNOW WHY	Her husband, handsome, young, muscled
LIVINIA	The young maid in the Paris hotel, perhaps attractive
THE PRINCE FOR ALL SEASONS	An arrogant prince
THE YOUNG BRIDE	The young bride of the prince, perhaps attractive
THE MAN IN THE BEAR SUIT	Weary, masculine, French
JOHNNY ROCKETS	A teen pop star, played by Dan
THE HOBBLED MAN	A hunchbacked recluse
WAITER	
HOTELIER	
CONSTABLE 1	
CONSTABLE 2	

Songs

(in order of appearance)

New Ways of Living

What Road

A Million Votes for Jenny O

Johnny Rockets' Song

Submarines Don't Mind

An Actor's Revenge

Daniel's Song

Don't Become The Thing You Hated

A Note on the Songs

Dan Bejar wrote eight original songs for *All Our Happy Days Are Stupid* after Sheila Heti sent him a draft of the play in 2002, with the agreement that he would write the music for the play. He sent back an audio tape of himself singing the songs, with no indication of where they should go or which character was to sing them. The songs were never incorporated into any of the workshops until the backyard reading organized by Jordan Tannahill. However, Chris Abraham, who directed the third workshop, suggested that there could be a separate character—Dan—who performed the songs. Heti incorporated this idea into the script, and placed the songs where they seemed to go. When it appeared that the play was not going to be produced, Bejar released a number of the songs on his 2004 album, *Your Blues*.

The songs can be listened to at sheilaheti.net/songs.

Original Cast & Production

DIRECTED BY JORDAN TANNAHILL WITH ERIN BRUBACHER
AT VIDEOFAG, IN TORONTO, OCTOBER 29 – NOVEMBER 3, 2013

LIGHTING DESIGNER	Zack Russell
STAGE MANAGER	Laura Hendrickson
SET DESIGNER	Rae Powell
COSTUME DESIGNER	Jordan Tannahill and company
PRODUCER	Renna Reddie
CARPENTER	Ben Carson
JENNY ODDI	Lorna Wright
MS. ODDI	Naomi Skwarna
MR. ODDI	Alexander Carson
DANIEL SING	Nick Hune-Brown
MRS. SING	Becky Johnson
MR. SING	Jon McCurley
DAN, JOHNNY ROCKETS	Henri Faberge
LIVINIA	Erin Brubacher
THE HANDSOME MAN WHO DOESN'T KNOW WHY, THE MAN IN THE BEAR SUIT	Michael McManus
THE PRINCE FOR ALL SEASONS	Carl Wilson
THE YOUNG BRIDE	Meghan Swaby
THE HOBBLED MAN, WAITER, CONSTABLE 1	Kayla Lorette
PLURABELLE, HOTELIER, CONSTABLE 2	Anne Wessels

WITH NANCY BOCOCK ON SAXOPHONE

2015 Cast & Production

DIRECTED BY JORDAN TANNAHILL WITH ERIN BRUBACHER
AT THE HARBOURFRONT CENTRE, IN TORONTO, FEBRUARY 11–14, 2015
AND THE KITCHEN, IN NEW YORK CITY, FEBRUARY 19–28, 2015

PRODUCTION MANAGER, LIGHTING DESIGNER	Zack Russell
STAGE MANAGER	Laura Hendrickson
SET DESIGNER	Rae Powell
COSTUME DESIGNER	Juliann Wilding
JENNY ODDI	Lorna Wright
MS. ODDI	Naomi Skwarna
MR. ODDI	Alexander Carson
DANIEL SING	Nick Hune-Brown
MRS. SING	Becky Johnson
MR. SING	Jon McCurley
DAN, JOHNNY ROCKETS	Henri Faberge
LIVINIA	Erin Brubacher
THE HANDSOME MAN WHO DOESN'T KNOW WHY, THE MAN IN THE BEAR SUIT	Michael McManus
THE PRINCE FOR ALL SEASONS	Carl Wilson
THE YOUNG BRIDE	Meghan Swaby
THE HOBBLED MAN, WAITER, CONSTABLE 1	Kayla Lorette
PLURABELLE, HOTELIER, CONSTABLE 2	Anne Wessels

PRODUCED AT THE KITCHEN BY SUBURBAN BEAST
IN ASSOCIATION WITH MCSWEENEY'S, WARBY PARKER,
AND THE HARBOURFRONT CENTRE

ACT I

A curtain hangs in front of the stage. DAN *stands facing it, his back to the audience, quietly playing his guitar and singing the final bars of "Don't Become The Thing You Hated." He may even have been playing when the audience came in. When he has finished singing, he turns to the audience. There is canned cheering, canned applause. He bows slightly, then turns around and pushes himself through the slit in the middle of the curtain.*

Late afternoon. A gaudy, bubble-gum Paris street scene. A parade is underway, perhaps with parade sounds. DAN, *still holding his guitar, loses himself in the crowd, while from the confusion emerge* JENNY, MS. ODDI, *and* MR. ODDI. *(Their last name is pronounced OH-dee.)*

JENNY: I think this must be the best day of my life. I'm not exaggerating. I always know when I'm having one of the best days of my life. I get a little feeling down inside of me—

MS. ODDI: All right. We've heard enough.

MR. ODDI: The more you talk about it the less true it will be.

JENNY: I don't find that at all. I find the more I talk about it the *more* true it will be. Talking about it makes it so!

MS. ODDI: Just watch the parade.

JENNY: *(crushed already)* It's awful being twelve. Really awful! Nothing you say is respected by anyone! If you could only see how much smarter than my friends I am, you would know.

MS. ODDI: Your friends are not the issue, Jenny. We think your friends are very nice.

JENNY: Sure! Nice! But just deny the fact that they are less intelligent than me!

MS. ODDI: I don't think about twelve-year-old girls in those terms! A twelve-year-old girl is a twelve-year-old girl, pure and simple. If you would like me to evaluate your friends, bring them back in five or six years. They're hardly on my radar.

JENNY: Well, if you could see what sort of fuss some of them cause on the street… In any case, you wouldn't be telling them to come back in five or six years.

MS. ODDI: How am I supposed to help it if some people are sick and perverted? Bystanders. I can't account for all bystanders!

MR. ODDI: Now, stop it you two. If you would only watch the parade.

JENNY: I hope we're not here for my benefit, because I really could care less about the parade. There are things I am much more interested in.

MR. ODDI: Who said we were here for your benefit? A parade is to everyone's benefit.

MS. ODDI: That's right. Do you think the lion appeals only to the very young? The lion is a sign of great strength. You know who has great strength? Your father.

JENNY: (scoffing) My father.

MR. ODDI: I'm going back to the hotel.

JENNY & MS. ODDI: Oh, don't go! Don't go!

MR. ODDI: Have you given one thought to whether or not this is any fun for me? Just standing here and standing here while you two bicker on? A lot of good that does for my health.

JENNY: We're not bickering.

MS. ODDI: I don't know how you expected it to go. Dragging us to a stupid parade. Is Jenny interested in some stupid parade? She's almost thirteen years old.

MR. ODDI: Let's go then.

JENNY: Please, let's not leave for my sake. I am perfectly happy to watch the stupid parade. You've taken me from all my friends; I don't see why I don't just lie down on the sidewalk and die.

MR. ODDI: (loudly) Then let's go for *my* sake. We're certainly not here for *my* benefit. Come on, no more discussion about it. We're going.

MS. ODDI: At last.

(*They start to walk.*)

JENNY: I was just dying in that sun.

MS. ODDI: Precisely. That sun was *terrible*.

MR. ODDI: If you have such a terrible time in the afternoon sun you should wear a sunhat.

MS. ODDI: I don't like to sweat.

JENNY: All the same; a sunhat saves the complexion.

MS. ODDI: I do not worry about my complexion. *You* should not be worrying about my complexion. My complexion is nobody's business but my own.

JENNY: Hey, wait a minute! I know that boy! He's from my school!

MS. ODDI: Where? Back home? What a thing!

JENNY: Imagine meeting him all the way in Paris!

(*JENNY pushes through the crowd to* DANIEL, *who stands with his parents,* MR. *and* MRS. SING.)

MR. ODDI: If you are going to say hello, be careful! Please, Jenny! You're not supposed to walk among the characters!

JENNY: Young Daniel!

DANIEL: Jenny! Jenny Oddi! Are you here in Paris too?

JENNY: I am!

DANIEL: Marvellous! I was just saying to my mother and father... Oh, wait a minute. Mother?

MRS. SING: Yes, Danny?

DANIEL: This is Jenny. She's in my class at school.

MRS. SING: From back home!

JENNY: Hello, Mrs. Sing.

MRS. SING: Hello.

DANIEL: This is my father.

MR. SING: Hello. *(awkward pause)* Jenny, are you travelling with your family in Paris?

JENNY: Yes, they're—

MR. SING: Danny tells us you're from his school.

JENNY: I am.

MRS. SING: Do you like it here?

JENNY: Sure. I like the women a lot. I think the older women are remarkable; so beautiful and well-dressed. A lifetime of having men look at you, don't you think? That's my mother's opinion of it. Makes a woman glow, she says.

MRS. SING: I don't agree at all. I think it is the weather.

DANIEL: Jenny has a special knowledge of the weather. She did a report last year on air currents.

JENNY: That's right. I forgot all about it.

DANIEL: It was good.

JENNY: It *was* good, it's true. But all in all, I never got into it. It was just research to the page.

DANIEL: What?

JENNY: Research to the page. Don't my mom and dad look so sad there? I'll get them.

(*She starts to go. Stops.*)

JENNY: Do you think it's right, all this stupid parading?

DANIEL: (*hesitates*) Right?

JENNY: In the streets of Paris! I had such a completely different vision of what it would be like here. I was always told that it was the most romantic city in the world. Lots of kissing, lovers holding hands, strolling down the avenues, but I haven't seen *any* of that! This ridiculous parade has been going on since we arrived and I'm sick of it! We keep running into it. My parents think it's amusing for me, but it's not. I think it's so limited. Wait.

(*JENNY goes to get her parents.*)

MRS. SING: (*disapproving*) She has such tiny hands!

(*JENNY returns with MR. and MS. ODDI.*)

JENNY: These are my parents. This is Daniel.

MS. ODDI: Hello Daniel.

DANIEL: Hi.

JENNY: And these are Daniel's parents, Mr. and Mrs. Sing.

MR. SING: Pleasure. Philip Sing. This is my wife, Joy.

MR. ODDI: Jack Oddi.

(The men shake hands.)

MRS. SING: *(to Ms. Oddi)* Your daughter goes to school with our Danny.

MS. ODDI: We were surprised to hear it. Imagine, meeting all the way in Paris!

MRS. SING: *(coldly)* Well, it *is* a small world. You must have realized that by now, Ms. Oddi.

MR. SING: *(gracious)* I imagine they must be good friends, to have recognized each other so quickly.

MRS. SING: I'd think so.

MS. ODDI: *(arrogant)* I wouldn't. Don't you remember when you were in school? At that age your world is so limited, you're intimate with the faces of everyone from the smallest grade to the highest.

MRS. SING: I disagree!

MS. ODDI: Well, Jenny tells me everything, and she told me just a few weeks ago that it is so *limited*, school is, and I believed her. Why shouldn't I? Because she's twelve? Just consider the facts. Two young people, all the way in Paris. If their outlooks were broader you'd think they would have completely overlooked each other. Or wouldn't even have been looking at all.

JENNY: I wasn't looking; I just noticed.

MRS. SING: *(to MS. ODDI)* I think you're confusing everything, if you don't mind me saying.

MS. ODDI: Say what you like!

(Silence.)

MS. ODDI: *(turning to her husband)* Let's go.

MR. ODDI: It was a pleasure meeting you.

MR. SING: Pleasure.

(The men shake hands. THE ODDIS turn to go.)

DANIEL: What? Are you going?

JENNY: I have to follow my parents now.

MS. ODDI: *(beckoning)* Jenny!

JENNY: *(to DANIEL)* I'm sorry about her. She always has to make a speech! What's so great about a speech?

MS. ODDI: When did I make a speech?

JENNY: Right now to his mother! Why can't you ever just shut up?

MS. ODDI: I didn't make a speech, and besides, even if I did. A speech explains what you're thinking. You'll understand it when you get a little older. As it is, you know little enough about such matters. You think it is sufficient just to say whatever gets stuck in your mind, then stand back and let someone *else* say the little things that pop in and out of *their* mind. It's fine enough for now, but soon your ideas will be more complicated and then you'll see very well the use of speeches. As it is, you're only twelve… *hopeless!* How can you be expected to understand anything?

MR. ODDI: Oh, Jenny makes her little speeches.

JENNY: Why do you have to say *little* speeches? Why use the word *little?* Why are you always trying to humiliate me?

MR. ODDI: I am not trying to humiliate you.

JENNY: *(to DANIEL)* I'm sorry.

(She hurries off after her parents, then turns and stops.)

MS. ODDI: Jenny!

JENNY: *(calling DANIEL)* Where are you staying?

DANIEL: I don't know… it's yellow. Where are you staying?

JENNY: I don't know. *(to her parents)* Where are we staying?

MR. ODDI: *(impatiently)* I have it written down in my book.

JENNY: Where's your book?

MS. ODDI: Jenny, come on!

JENNY: *(to DANIEL, calling)* Near the parade!

(THE ODDIS and JENNY exit.)

MR. SING: They seem like a very decent family.

MRS. SING: I hope you're joking.

MR. SING: I was *not* joking.

MRS. SING: The mother was very rude to me.

MR. SING: Please don't start with your evil eyes.

MRS. SING: What evil eyes? I have not started.

MR. SING: Once you start with those evil eyes the day is ruined!

DANIEL: Yes Mom, please don't.

MRS. SING: I am not starting with the evil eyes!

MR. SING: I don't see why I brought you to Paris. I should have just left you at home. There you could make your evil eyes at Mrs. Lau, you could make your evil eyes at the dog all day long. We wouldn't have had to worry about it all the way in Paris!

MRS. SING: Oh yes? Well, if you had left me at home who would have looked after Daniel while you spent all last night in the lap of some exotic dancer?

MR. SING: He should not be hearing this!

MRS. SING: He will have to hear this! What kind of man his father is…

(DANIEL *starts walking away.*)

MR. SING: Daniel—come back! Daniel! Don't get lost in the crowd!

(He does.)

MRS. SING: You spent all night licking her on her leg, and then you returned home to me as though I was supposed to bare my leg for you!

MR. SING: Please, I don't want to get into it. It was your idea.

MRS. SING: Only to make you happy. *(looks around)* Daniel! Daniel!

(DAN emerges. He resembles DANIEL. He will reappear throughout the play to sing with his guitar; the players never notice or acknowledge him. He begins to sing as THE SINGS argue more quietly.)

"New Ways of Living"

Maybe I should have loved you...
Maybe I should have sworn
Not to be born
Of this wretched glove too soon
But a dragon needs room
But a dragon needs room
To run run run run

(Suddenly, MR. SING realizes that his son is gone. The music continues under this exchange.)

MR. SING: It was supposed to be different! Daniel? Look, we've lost Daniel.

MRS. SING: No we haven't. Daniel! Daniel!

(*THE SINGS look for DANIEL in the crowd while DAN continues to sing, nonchalant.*)

"New Ways of Living" (*cont'd*)

Treacherous fop don't be embarrassed
For looking good at your table on the terrace
That you call home
I'm sold
Paris, London, Rome's too young for you
And your kind
Explosions want to see what they can find
New ways of living…
It's you and your kind
The new ways of living
It's you and your kind
The new ways of living
It's you and your kind
The new ways of living
It's you and your kind
The new ways of living
All right

Dining room of the hotel. Next morning. MR. ODDI *looks at a map.* JENNY
looks worriedly into a newspaper. MS. ODDI *is eating her breakfast, putting
jam on things. The music from the previous scene continues in this one,*
DAN *now in the dining room, at another table.*

"New Ways of Living" *(cont'd)*

It's you and your kind
The new ways of living *(x 4)*

JENNY: They still haven't found Daniel.

MS. ODDI: I think it's very irresponsible of that woman to lose her son
in the parade. Jack, have we ever lost Jenny?

MR. ODDI: We have *never* lost Jenny!

JENNY: It's sad, that's all. I see him, a friend from school, and the
next thing—I'm reading in the paper that a boy from Cedervale has
gone missing in that stupid parade! Dad, if you had told me Paris had
parades all summer I never would have thought it was a good idea to
come. Really, I wanted something authentic!

MS. ODDI: Isn't this butter authentic?

JENNY: Yes, I suppose the butter is authentic.

MS. ODDI: Then I don't see what you're complaining about. You want to live in a world of absolute purity. That's nonsense! You have to get your head together in time for grade seven! Do you want all the older boys laughing at you? Well, they will if you go around talking about authenticity all the time. The world is the world. You can't divide it up like that!

MR. ODDI: If Jenny wanted your opinion she would have asked for it! All she's saying is that she doesn't like the parade. I can understand that. It swallowed up her friend.

MS. ODDI: Well then, I suppose there's nothing to say.

JENNY: I'm sure I could find him if I looked.

MS. ODDI: (*contemptuously*) Why? Because you're twelve and he's twelve?

JENNY: It has nothing to do with that.

MS. ODDI: You are too romantic a girl!

JENNY: We have an understanding. A mutual sympathy. For instance—

MS. ODDI: (*disgusted*) Please Jenny, we don't want to hear about your understanding.

JENNY: I was going to be polite.

MS. ODDI: Some things are best left to the imagination.

JENNY: All right! Leave it to the imagination, then!

MS. ODDI: You ought to spend your time thinking about other things. You ought to be taking a look at the world around you! As it is you're like a six-year-old, completely self-involved.

(*Pause.*)

JENNY: I think it's just terrible.

MR. ODDI: You are so fond of people.

MS. ODDI: Pass the jam.

JENNY: It's right by your elbow! (*after a pause*) I am going off on my own today.

MR. ODDI: You can't. You're too young, obviously. Even you know it.

JENNY: I'll take the phone and you can call me all day if that's what it takes!

MS. ODDI: That is not what it takes, Jenny. It takes five or six years of maturity. You don't know how to look at things in the right way. You're always in a muddle. That boy you think is your friend? Well, was it very friendly to get lost and separated from his family?

JENNY: I suppose it wasn't. But I'm sure on the other hand it had nothing to do with him. He was probably just looking at one of the characters when his parents wandered off.

MS. ODDI: I've come to expect more from you.

MR. ODDI: Leave her alone. She's upset.

MS. ODDI: All right.

JENNY: No. She doesn't have to leave me alone either. *(with difficulty)* I'm not upset.

MR. ODDI: Come, come. Obviously you're upset. Look at you! Look at you!

MS. ODDI: Yes, look at you! You have a tear in your eye!

JENNY: I am trying to hold it in.

MS. ODDI: Well you're doing a terrible job! Let it out, Jenny, you're not proving anything.

MR. ODDI: She's upset, Grace. Leave her alone.

JENNY: I'm going to go lie down.

MR. ODDI: If you lie down you're going to miss the day. Do you want to miss the whole day?

JENNY: I don't want to miss the whole day but I do want to lie down.

MS. ODDI: Well, I think it's fine. Go lie down, Jenny. But just for ten minutes. We'll be waiting here to leave in ten minutes. You have a little rest.

JENNY: Thank you.

MS. ODDI: It's difficult. Daniel was your friend.

JENNY: I know.

MS. ODDI: You're very sensitive.

(JENNY *leaves.* MR. *and* MS. ODDI *look at each other.* MS. ODDI *sighs.*)

MS. ODDI: I don't know. She's a very sensitive girl.

MR. ODDI: She's just like you were when you were twelve.

MS. ODDI: You did not know me when I was twelve.

MR. ODDI: How I imagine you to have been.

MS. ODDI: You could imagine me one of a hundred different ways. What would it have to do with anything? Jenny's upset! About her little friend, Daniel!

MR. ODDI: I really can't take this anymore.

(*He returns to his map.*)

MS. ODDI: That's right. Look at your map! As if the key to life were in your map!

MR. ODDI: Can't we please have a pleasant breakfast?

MS. ODDI: That's what I asked you this very morning, coming down the stairs. Don't you remember?

MR. ODDI: You would see if you only looked around that there are a dozen other families right here in this very room and all of them are having pleasant breakfasts. Not one of them is running off in tears!

MS. ODDI: I don't care to look at a bunch of other families who all smell bad in their own ways. Have you ever noticed that, Jack? How bad other families smell?

MR. ODDI: Sure. Remember Irene?

MS. ODDI: Yes! Irene Melo! Then you see what I'm speaking of. Phew! If that house didn't stink! Like onions and sweat and soil.

MR. ODDI: Don't start showing off.

MS. ODDI: What?

MR. ODDI: Please stop showing off! "Like onions and sweat and soil." You're not a poet, Grace.

MS. ODDI: *(hurt)* I'm not trying to be a poet.

MR. ODDI: ...trying to describe the way things are. Leave that to the poets... for heaven's sake, Grace!

MS. ODDI: I was just searching for the words.

MR. ODDI: A poet doesn't search for the words, just ladies trying to look all poetical!

MS. ODDI: *(still hurt)* You're wrong. Poets *do* search for the words. They search for the words in every lyric.

MR. ODDI: *(looking back at his map)* You have no idea what you're talking about.

MS. ODDI: Maybe I don't.

(No response.)

MS. ODDI: I'd like you to be more tender, Jack. Just a little. While we're on vacation.

MR. ODDI: We should have gotten our own room.

MS. ODDI: It was expensive…

(MS. ODDI sighs. A pause.)

MS. ODDI: I once knew a little Japanese boy, when I was in school. He did everything wrong, backwards. When everyone else was wearing their pants with the zipper in front, he would wear his with the zipper in the back. Instead of eating, he threw up every lunchtime. No one thought it was peculiar. He came from the other side of the world, after all. Well, that's all I remember of him. Just weird. Playful, too. If you can call one child playful… among the many.

(She sighs. She picks up the paper and reads, in a distracted manner. Into the dining room come MR. and MRS. SING. MS. ODDI notices them. THE SINGS go and sit down at their table.)

MS. ODDI: *(leaning over, whispering to MR. ODDI)* It's those parents! The parents who lost the boy! We met them yesterday. The Sings!

MR. ODDI: *(interested)* I remember.

MS. ODDI: Should we go over and say hi?

MR. ODDI: I don't know.

(They watch them.)

MR. ODDI: Yes, let's try it.

MS. ODDI: But what if they're too upset to be friendly? I would hate for them to be mean to me.

MR. ODDI: Come on, they won't be mean to you. They know our daughter.

MS. ODDI: Right.

(They stand up and go over, carefully.)

MR. ODDI: Hello, Mr. and Mrs. Sing. We met you yesterday with our daughter, Jenny.

MR. SING: Oh, hello.

(MRS. SING looks up coldly, then goes on with her breakfast.)

MR. ODDI: Imagine… staying at the same hotel!

MR. SING: We like this hotel very much.

MR. ODDI: So do we.

MS. ODDI: I like the decor.

MR. ODDI: My wife is very particular about decor.

MS. ODDI: I think a building *ought* to have decor. Some call it a sense of place, others call it a sense of perspective. Either way, you must agree that it gives you a vantage to look out over the world from; a vantage that's often lost when travelling, when you're without a bit of your routine. So yes, I like the curtains they've chosen for this room, and that they thought of it. It makes it a little more like home.

MR. SING: Well, thank you for stopping by.

MR. ODDI: We're sorry about Daniel.

MR. SING: *(awkwardly)* Well… thank you.

(Pause.)

MS. ODDI: Good-bye.

(They walk away.)

MR. ODDI: *(hissing, quiet)* You were very rude.

MS. ODDI: *(astonished)* How?

MR. ODDI: I'm embarrassed to be your husband. I won't go any further than that.

MS. ODDI: What happened?

MR. ODDI: *(gritting his teeth)* How can you go on making pleasantries when their son is dead?

MS. ODDI: He's not dead. He's missing.

MR. ODDI: A fair bit of difference that makes to the parents! When a child is missing a child is dead!

MS. ODDI: What do you know? You exaggerate.

MR. ODDI: I know these things, Grace.

MS. ODDI: You think you know everything because you read magazines. Well, a magazine can't tell you about the heart, Jack, as much as you'd like it to. For that there's only fiction. Books!

MR. ODDI: I am speaking about your behavior! Don't bring up magazines.

MS. ODDI: Well my behavior is not up for conversation! I put a stop to it! It is not up for conversation!

MR. ODDI: I will tell Jenny this. I will tell her of how you have behaved. Then she will be ashamed to have a mother!

(*He goes back to his map.* MR. SING *comes over.*)

MS. ODDI: Mr. Sing!

MR. SING: I am sorry to bother you, but may we borrow the sugar? We won't be a moment with it.

MS. ODDI: Oh yes! Oh yes, of course! Please, have the sugar. Take it. Keep it! We don't need it back!

MR. SING: Thank you.

MS. ODDI: (*calling after him as he retreats to his table*) We don't need it!

MR. ODDI: (*nodding approvingly*) That was good of you.

MS. ODDI: I thought: We need the sugar, but they need it more.

(MR. ODDI *keeps reading his map.*)

MS. ODDI: (*smiling, satisfied*) "We need it, but they need it more."

(JENNY *enters, a little disheveled, as if having woken from a nap.*)

JENNY: I'm ready to go.

MS. ODDI: (*excited*) Ready?

JENNY: I said I'm ready. You're just repeating me now.

(MR. ODDI *folds up his map.*)

MR. ODDI: You'll be happy to know I have figured out our day. Ready and set?

JENNY: Oh, there are the Sings!

(JENNY *wanders over to them, uncertain.*)

MS. ODDI: (*calling after her, warning*) It's a very difficult situation, Jenny.

JENNY: Mr. and Mrs. Sing?

(MRS. SING *looks up.*)

MR. SING: Hello, Jenny.

JENNY: Would you like to… I was wondering if you'd like to come around with me and my family today?

MR. SING: No thank you, Jenny. We're going to stay by the hotel and wait for Daniel.

JENNY: I just thought that if we all went together, it would be a nicer day, for the company.

MRS. SING: I don't want to say it, Jenny, but your mother is very irritating to me and I am just in no mood.

JENNY: *(weakly)* But when people come together—

MRS. SING: You are a very pushy girl! We are going to stay in our room and wait for Daniel! Our son has gone missing and we love him very much! *(begins crying)* I don't want to be rude but we are in no mood to go off with your family today! We don't know if we'll ever see him again!

JENNY: I think you *will* see him again.

MRS. SING: What do you know! You're only twelve! There is nothing stupider, I repeat nothing stupider, than being twelve!

MR. SING: Today is not a good day, Jenny.

(JENNY turns to go. She returns to her parents.)

MS. ODDI: Come. You shouldn't have created a scene.

(She puts her arm around JENNY.)

JENNY: I'm sorry.

MS. ODDI: You thought your charm could take care of it all, but that is not always the case. Even for girls with whom it *is* always the case, they are generally much prettier than you are. One day it will be easier, when you have wit, and that day will come in its own time, but not until you know a little more about the world first. As it stands, you are very naive. *(shrill)* A great naïf!

MR. ODDI: That's enough for today. The day has just begun and we are already two hours into a lecture! Can't we please just try to be happy?

MS. ODDI: You and I discussed this, Jack. If you were completely uninterested in the educational aspect of this trip you should have laid that out before we left and I would have stayed at home. I have little enough time for fun. Jenny will be thirteen in May!

JENNY: I'll learn!

(They all go.)

MRS. SING: *(appalled)* What an astonishing woman!

Parisian park. Early that afternoon. THE ODDI FAMILY *sits on a bench, distracted. The parade is still going on.*

MR. ODDI: I know you were saying this the other day, Jenny, and I think you were right. Why all the revellers? Where is the wine?

JENNY: Thank you, father.

MR. ODDI: In fact, if it would not be going too far, I think Cedervale is more like Paris than Paris itself, and I will be happy and relieved when we get back. Think even of the striped umbrellas at the beach where we go sometimes, for instance!

MS. ODDI: Jack, if you're going to go and say that, you might as well just throw in the towel right now and all of us with it. There's nothing like a quitter! *(more hysterical)* And there's the gutter!

MR. ODDI: Calm down, Grace. *(looking at the map)* Now look here, I think I've found the spot, pinpointed it. It's not two miles off, in that direction.

(He points.)

MR. ODDI: *(to JENNY, a little hyper)* You want authentic Parisian life? You'd like Papa to take you there today?

(THE MAN IN THE BEAR SUIT *comes over. He speaks with an exaggerated, phony French accent.*)

THE MAN IN THE BEAR SUIT: Hello little girl!

JENNY: *(looks up, sarcastic)* Thank you very much for calling me a little girl. I'm twelve years old, you know.

MS. ODDI: Twelve years old is still little. Have you even gotten your period yet? I bet not!

THE MAN IN THE BEAR SUIT: Wouldn't you like to join the parade, see what it's like to be on parade?

JENNY: No thank you. I think your parade is ridiculous! It is absolutely ruining Paris for me, and my mother, and my father!

MR. ODDI: *(turning)* We do not find it very Parisian.

THE MAN IN THE BEAR SUIT: Oh, but it *is* Parisian! France has a great comedic tradition, you know, and it was not at all unusual in the 1400s, for example, to have jesters walking through the streets, in costumes much like this one… or this one. No, do not think the French courts dismissed peasant humor. In fact, court life would have been all intrigues and murders if the lightheartedness of the circus performers wasn't there to intervene! I don't speak from personal experience, but I have done my reading, and I know for sure.

MR. ODDI: You can keep your bugger history! We just don't find it very sophisticated!

THE MAN IN THE BEAR SUIT: Monsieur, I understand. When I first moved to Paris seven years ago, I had a very different idea of how it would turn out for me. I came with little money, only one change of clothes. I was young. I thought I'd paint the Seine, yes, sit along the water all day, and in the night proposition women for threesomes or foursomes—

MS. ODDI: Excuse me! She is twelve years old!

THE MAN IN THE BEAR SUIT: But she must know what it is, a threesome.

JENNY: I know what it is.

MR. ODDI: Would you leave my family in peace!

THE MAN IN THE BEAR SUIT: Indulging in threesomes is very good. They're a pleasure.

MS. ODDI: Anyone can see they're a pleasure!

THE MAN IN THE BEAR SUIT: Especially with two men. Then the possibilities are even more interesting.

(MR. ODDI *gets up and punches* THE MAN IN THE BEAR SUIT *in the face. He staggers back.* MR. ODDI *turns away but then* THE MAN IN THE BEAR SUIT *returns the punch.*)

JENNY: Oh, stop! Just stop! Will you please stop it!

(*The two men back off each other.*)

JENNY: Father, really!

(THE MAN IN THE BEAR SUIT *wanders off.*)

MS. ODDI: Are you hurt?

MR. ODDI: I'm not hurt, Grace, thank you very much.

(*He rubs his hand.* JENNY *starts to cry.*)

MR. ODDI: See what you've done? You've startled her.

JENNY: Do you think they'll ever find him, really?

MS. ODDI: Well, Jenny, it's unlikely. It is *very* unlikely.

JENNY: Perhaps he really was taken. And if he was?

MS. ODDI: If he was, then we probably won't see him again. Adults who take children tend to make all they can of the opportunity, and that does not include returning them to their parents.

JENNY: (*crying*) Poor Daniel!

MR. ODDI: Now, Jenny. Let's try and forget all about this. Have I something to show the two of you! A real French Parisian district, with real Parisians going about their daily business.

JENNY: I want to go back to the hotel with the Sings!

MR. ODDI: I am not going to ruin your mother's whole day on account of your wanting to go back. We'll go back to the hotel in the evening, and we'll help the Sings then. There's not much to be done about it now.

JENNY: Don't you care about Daniel?

MR. ODDI: Of course I care, Jenny, but he's not our son and there's nothing we can do about it. We're not the guilty party.

MS. ODDI: (*saying it, but distracted*) That's right, Jenny. Don't start treating your father like he's the guilty party. Your father spent a lot of money getting us over here, and while we're here, we should be out, not just sitting in a hotel with the Sings.

JENNY: Perhaps they need our company.

MS. ODDI: If they do, they'll just have to wait until we get back for dinner tonight.

MR. ODDI: They're not waiting around for us now. Don't be ridiculous. They're not sitting there thinking, "Oh, where are the Oddis, our only friends in the world?" Be reasonable, Jenny.

MS. ODDI: Yes. Come along. Your father has planned a really nice day and we're going to see it through.

MR. ODDI: That's right… a real Parisian district. We might even hear some French!

Hotel lobby. Later that afternoon. MR. *and* MRS. SING *sit on a bench.*

MRS. SING: It seemed like they might be our friends, the Oddis, the way they came over to our table this morning and then gave us the sugar. I really could see it, I thought—yes! In her face was something of the brutal woman. I do like brutal women. I have all along, since I was a girl! Oh, think of it. I would just admire her... sit and admire her and stare. And she would admire me, too! And we'd just talk about all the little things in the world...

MR. SING: You snubbed her. She was being perfectly friendly and you were rude.

MRS. SING: I don't even remember.

MR. SING: You are *always* rude.

MRS. SING: Perhaps I was brought up that way...

MR. SING: You cannot blame your mother and father who are twenty years dead!

(Pause.)

MRS. SING: But it was almost a betrayal, wasn't it? For them to go like that? I thought they might turn around and come back to us as soon as they stepped out that door. I kept watching the door... like a little animal.

MR. SING: They wanted to see the sights.

MRS. SING: Yes! Like us! We wanted to see the sights, too!

MR. SING: We'll see the sights next time!

MRS. SING: All I wanted was to spend one day in the shops, but I didn't want to tell you. I had it in mind to buy a nice dress, only one, but which I could bring back and tell Mrs. Lau: *This is from Paris. This is a Paris original!*

MR. SING: I don't know why you are always trying to make Mrs. Lau jealous. She is an illiterate cleaning-woman. You have never had any ambition!

MRS. SING: No, it's true. I don't know why I thought it would be a good idea.

MR. SING: What you want is always nothing but trouble, that's what I think.

MRS. SING: I should just throw myself into the river. With my ribbons and my robes.

MR. SING: Don't talk nonsense.

MRS. SING: I'm nothing but a burden to you.

MR. SING: You say it but you don't mean it. (*pause*) You don't have ribbons and you only have one robe.

(*THE ODDIS enter, exhausted after a long day.*)

MRS. SING: (*whispering*) Look, it's the Oddis! Sit up!

(*THE ODDIS approach but JENNY runs ahead.*)

JENNY: Have they found Daniel yet?

MR. SING: No, Jenny, they have not.

MR. ODDI: We're so sorry.

MS. ODDI: Yes, yes, so sorry.

MR. SING: Yes...

MRS. SING: And how did you spend your day?

MR. ODDI: We looked for Daniel all over.

JENNY: (*desperate*) No, we did not. They wouldn't let me go to the park. I told them I wanted to feed the birds—but it wasn't true! I thought we'd see Daniel there! I know he loves birds, and I thought maybe he would follow the little pigeons in...

MS. ODDI: She's confused. We kept our eye out for him all day.

MRS. SING: (*touching the arm of MS. ODDI's blouse*) Ms. Oddi, may I speak with you confidentially?

MS. ODDI: I... don't think so.

MRS. SING: No?

MS. ODDI: Whatever you want to say to me, you can say before my husband, and Jenny.

(MRS. SING *sits silent.*)

MRS. SING: Please, we won't go far. Just… over there… by the tree.

MS. ODDI: (*glances at it*) All right.

(*They go over to stand by the plastic tree.*)

MRS. SING: (*giggling, then bringing her hand up to her mouth*) I don't know what's come over me! I don't know what's wrong with me! (*bursts into tears*) Oh, it's just been such a terrible day! You have never lost a child, have you, Ms. Oddi?

MS. ODDI: Never.

MRS. SING: It's not like you imagine it. You find that even oranges look menacing to you. The whole world turns inside-out, and you see nothing but the maggots! The midgets and the maggots!

MS. ODDI: I wouldn't know about that, Mrs. Sing. I have always tried to look on the bright side of things.

MRS. SING: Me too, me too. Not the midgets. Oh, Ms. Oddi, I have a feeling we could understand each other!

MS. ODDI: No, I'm sorry, Mrs. Sing. You have the wrong idea about me. I don't know how I ever gave you that idea, but I like the comforts of my family, and the few friends I have are enough for me.

MRS. SING: But you are a passionate woman… in some ways?

(MS. ODDI notices JENNY playing with the leaves of a hotel plant.)

MS. ODDI: Jenny! Stop that! Jenny's up to no good again. Please excuse me, Mrs. Sing. I hope they find Daniel.

(She steps away, pulling JENNY with her.)

MRS. SING: Please don't misunderstand me!

The hotel room of THE ODDIS. Early evening.

MR. ODDI: *(proudly)* Your mother plays the flute!

JENNY: What? I never knew that.

MR. ODDI: Listen to her. Come, Grace. *(to JENNY)* She brought it with her.

(MS. ODDI produces her flute.)

MS. ODDI: I sing, too.

JENNY: Impossible. How come I was never told?

MR. ODDI: We wanted it to be a surprise.

(MS. ODDI plays a note.)

MR. ODDI: Divine.

(MS. ODDI plays a whole song. When she is done, she holds her flute to her chest and smiles. MR. ODDI stands and claps, beaming.)

MR. ODDI: Marvellous! Marvellous! Isn't your mother incredible?

MS. ODDI: *(happily embarrassed)* Oh stop it.

(She quickly puts the flute away.)

MR. ODDI: Come.

(MS. ODDI *goes and sits beside her husband, who puts his arm tight around her waist and smiles. They sit there like that.*)

JENNY: Excuse me.

MS. ODDI: What is it, Jenny?

JENNY: I would like to talk to the police.

MR. ODDI: Oh Jenny, can't it wait?

MS. ODDI: Jenny, we are trying to have a nice time.

(*There is a knocking on the door.* THE ODDIS *look at each other questioningly.* JENNY *goes to answer it. Standing in the doorway are* PLURABELLE, *an older woman with an air of authority, and* THE HANDSOME MAN WHO DOESN'T KNOW WHY. *They push in.*)

PLURABELLE: Ms. Oddi.

MS. ODDI: Yes?

PLURABELLE: We understand you play the flute.

MR. ODDI: Were you spying?

PLURABELLE: Livinia was.

(LIVINIA *enters, hesitantly, then curtseys.*)

MR. ODDI: What does it matter? Is that not allowed in this hotel?

PLURABELLE: (*without enthusiasm*) Contrary, Sir. It's encouraged.

MS. ODDI: Then I don't see what I've done wrong.

PLURABELLE: We would like to invite you to dinner.

MS. ODDI: (*coldly*) We have eaten already, thank you.

PLURABELLE: Not as a guest. Tonight there will be a great honor for the hotel. The Prince For All Seasons will be dining here with his entourage and new bride. We have never had such a great honor, not since the hotel opened in 1748. Do you know what happened in 1748, Ms. Oddi?

JENNY: I do.

PLURABELLE & JENNY: (*in a rush*) In 1784 the Hoteliers Association of Western Europe produced an edict!

PLURABELLE: Don't speak out of turn! We were the first hotel to open under the regulations of that edict, which had four main points, and it was then that the King of Verdun honored us with a visit with his entourage and new bride! We were humbled and we served him a roast. It was delicious and everyone was satisfied. The only person who was not satisfied was his young bride. She took to her bed ill that night, and when she woke, she was dead.

MR. ODDI: Then she didn't wake. If she was dead.

PLURABELLE: Did I say woke? I meant "in the morning."

THE HANDSOME MAN: Tell her about the second honor.

PLURABELLE: *(shrill)* You are wrong! The second honor is tonight! Ms. Oddi, can we count on your participation?

MS. ODDI: You want me to play the flute?

PLURABELLE: We do.

MS. ODDI: Well… I am flattered, of course.

PLURABELLE: We will leave you to talk it over with each other. A husband and wife must consult on every detail, or else the marriage may go to pot. Have you found that?

MR. ODDI: No.

PLURABELLE: *(beckoning to THE HANDSOME MAN)* My husband will stay. When you have come to your decision, tell him, and he will inform me. We would be so honored. *(bowing as she exits)* Your notes are honeyed, Ms. Oddi, absolutely honeyed. And you are a vision of loveliness.

MS. ODDI: *(swallowing, quietly)* Thank you.

(PLURABELLE and LIVINIA leave. JENNY checks the door, opening it a little and looking out, then closing it.)

JENNY: The old one is waiting outside the door.

THE HANDSOME MAN: *(smiling)* She doesn't trust me.

(MS. ODDI turns to her husband with a hopeful, expectant look.)

MR. ODDI: Come on, it sounds ludicrous!

MS. ODDI: I don't know… I think it's quite an honor. To be asked. I am not even a professional.

MR. ODDI: We have tickets to a play. Don't you remember?

MS. ODDI: (scoffing) A play. (to THE HANDSOME MAN) Tell her I will.

THE HANDSOME MAN: It's a choice you both should agree on, don't you think? Or do you want to make your husband upset?

MR. ODDI: Yes, he's perfectly right. I think I should be included in the decision.

MS. ODDI: You won't let me? Why?

THE HANDSOME MAN: Often, Ma'am, it seems a husband doesn't like his wife to shine. I can't figure it myself. Who else should a man want to shine but his very own wife?

MR. ODDI: It has nothing to do with that! I am perfectly happy to see my wife shine!

THE HANDSOME MAN: You aren't hiding her light under a bushel? She's a beautiful woman, if you don't mind me saying, your wife is, and she would make the Prince very happy.

MR. ODDI: (to MS. ODDI) This is what you want?

JENNY: She's still there.

THE HANDSOME MAN: She's just spying on me. Keeps me on a short leash. Thinks I'm going to run around on her. (smiles)

MS. ODDI: I want to do it. I want it. I want it, Jack!

MR. ODDI: Well, you're being very irrational. That's all I can say.

MS. ODDI: I'm guided by my emotions this time!

MR. ODDI: Go ahead then.

MS. ODDI: (to THE HANDSOME MAN) Yes!

THE HANDSOME MAN: We're much obliged to you, Ma'am. You may not realize it, but it's quite an honor to be asked, and tonight will be the best night of your life, if you don't mind me hyperventilating.

MR. ODDI: (impatient) You mean hyperbolizing.

THE HANDSOME MAN: Your husband's a good man. Takes good care of you. He's no fool.

(He waits, looking at them.)

THE HANDSOME MAN: Well, good-bye.

(He goes. JENNY open the door for him and closes it behind him. We can hear a grunt of delight from PLURABELLE from behind the door. JENNY checks.)

JENNY: They're gone.

(MS. ODDI stands up in rapture. She begins pacing around the room impatiently, eagerly.)

MS. ODDI: Oh! Oh! I don't know what to say! *(turning to MR. ODDI)* I don't know what to say!

MR. ODDI: I don't know.

MS. ODDI: It really is an honor! At first I thought they were just saying that, I was suspicious. But I feel it in my bones. The Prince! The Prince For All Seasons… And his lovely young bride. How romantic!

MR. ODDI: See, it all sounds like a load of crap to me.

MS. ODDI: Must you spoil everything good in my life! For once *I* am the one who is necessary. I am the one who will make the evening shine! That man was right. You're jealous of me. You want to keep me tucked away in this hotel room, away from the eyes of the world. Why didn't I get on the stage? Why didn't I pursue my flute? Instead I took care of Jenny.

MR. ODDI: You worked.

MS. ODDI: I worked. Later. Yes, I did work. But never to my potential.

MR. ODDI: I coached you for interviews.

MS. ODDI: You helped in your own way.

MR. ODDI: *(angry)* Then?

MS. ODDI: But you never went out of your way to help! *(bursts into tears)* I have hidden my talent under a bushel.

MR. ODDI: You never professed an interest.

MS. ODDI: No, not out loud.

JENNY: *(more quietly than usual)* I never knew about it.

MS. ODDI: I was ashamed. It seemed frivolous.

MR. ODDI: Well it is, a little, unless you take it seriously. *(standing)* I'm not going to miss the theatre.

MS. ODDI: I know. *(sadly)* I can't really expect you to be proud of me, not even the tiniest bit… not if I never professed an interest. I have to practice. I only know one song. Take Jenny! I have no time to waste. I must rehearse!

MR. ODDI: I don't want you getting too carried away, is all. Don't forget the rest of your life!

MS. ODDI: No, it's true. The rest of my life is very important.

(MR. ODDI puts on his coat.)

MR. ODDI: Don't go changing your look. Your look is a good one.

MS. ODDI: *(nervously)* Is it?

MR. ODDI: You see? Keep it in proportion! Come along, Jenny. We're not missing the play. Don't forget your coat.

(MR. ODDI and JENNY leave. MS. ODDI lifts her flute to her lips and blows. There is not a pleasant sound. She looks at her flute in despair.)

SCENE 6

In the garden of the hotel. THE HANDSOME MAN WHO DOESN'T KNOW WHY *is looking lovingly at* LIVINIA, *a servant girl with long hair. He holds her in his arms.*

THE HANDSOME MAN: Tonight we will go from here…

LIVINIA: Yes.

THE HANDSOME MAN: My very own love.

LIVINIA: Oh, yes.

THE HANDSOME MAN: And you will be mine. In a little house by the woods. And there will be no man happier than I.

(They kiss. DAN *comes on, serenades them.)*

"What Road"

Once I was made beautiful in the light of an hour
But this year, I'm just a meal laid out for August to devour
So quick let's go, it's time for a ride
The future's yours, no way to lie
It is not yours, it is a replica of scattered ash
And the road the rain's on
What road, what road, what road, what road…

JENNY *and* MR. ODDI *flag a taxi in front of the hotel.* THE PRINCE FOR
ALL SEASONS *and* THE YOUNG BRIDE *are escorted by* PLURABELLE *into the
dining room.* MS. ODDI *exits her hotel room and heads for the dining room.
As all this happens, a sort of night scene occurs, where people assemble
themselves into where they are meant to be and* DAN *continues to sing.*

"What Road" *(cont'd)*

Able willing ready

Fuck the Spiral Jetty

Today we work large we aim high

To the spirit's sky designed to come down

On everyone at once

So quick let's go, it's time for a ride

The future's yours, no way to lie

It is not yours, it is a replica of scattered ash

And the road the rain's on

What road, what road, what road, what road…

SCENE 8

Private dining room in the hotel. THE PRINCE FOR ALL SEASONS *and* THE
YOUNG BRIDE *sit at an elaborate table.* PLURABELLE *stands back, beaming,
while* LIVINIA *serves.* MS. ODDI *stands off a bit, playing her flute rather
badly. She is near tears. She continues to play throughout the scene, and is
completely ignored.* DAN *continues to sing.*

"What Road" *(cont'd)*

I's been, working on some open-ended shit

I was looking for an in and that was it

Back at the recital

Signs remain vital

A statue of stone which rejects its own pulse

Your heart's square, your heart's fair, your heart's
     not even there

Wasting surely on the girls from Point Saint Clair

There is a light and it goes out, a…

Touch of classicism in the night

Your backlash was right where I wanted you

Yes, that's right, I wanted you

Yes, that's right, I wanted you

THE YOUNG BRIDE: I tried my best. Now I am recovered. I lay in my bed all day and Livinia attended to me.

THE PRINCE FOR ALL SEASONS: Who is Livinia?

THE YOUNG BRIDE: She is!

(LIVINIA *passes by to serve them another dish.*)

THE PRINCE FOR ALL SEASONS: You helped my young bride—now she is well! Before she was dying. She had fallen from her horse.

LIVINIA: I saw the spot on her head, Prince.

THE PRINCE FOR ALL SEASONS: She tells me it was you who made her better. That without you she might not have been made better at all.

LIVINIA: I don't know.

THE PRINCE FOR ALL SEASONS: Has no one taught you to be proud?

LIVINIA: Never.

THE PRINCE FOR ALL SEASONS: Then how can you possibly be happy?

LIVINIA: I am not.

THE PRINCE FOR ALL SEASONS: Then what good is your life! What good is your life if you are not proud, and therefore not happy? Is there not only one Livinia in this hotel?

LIVINIA: I am the only one.

THE PRINCE FOR ALL SEASONS: Then you must hold your head up high!

LIVINIA: I suppose.

THE PRINCE FOR ALL SEASONS: I will see to it that you do! You have nursed my beautiful young bride back to health… so I will not have you walking around this hotel alone, staring gloomily at the world, serving and cleaning up without any dignity of your own, when you are obviously remarkable!

LIVINIA: Thank you, Prince. It is too much what you say.

THE PRINCE FOR ALL SEASONS: But not at all. Do you have an education?

LIVINIA: Yes.

THE PRINCE FOR ALL SEASONS: What grade?

LIVINIA: Seventh grade, Prince. After that I was put to work and I have worked ever since.

THE PRINCE FOR ALL SEASONS: It is atrocious!

LIVINIA: Thank you. I was very good at school. I excelled.

THE PRINCE FOR ALL SEASONS: I am sure you did. You must become a tutor. The tutor of my young bride. I have been thinking of acquiring for her an education. She likes you.

THE YOUNG BRIDE: I was nearly dead. You saved me.

LIVINIA: *(curtseys)* Thank you, Princess.

THE PRINCE FOR ALL SEASONS: Call for me the woman who employs you.

LIVINIA: *(turning)* Plurabelle!

PLURABELLE: *(rushing over)* Is everything to your liking?

THE PRINCE FOR ALL SEASONS: I have been in conversation with your maid. She took care of my bride. When we arrived she was half-dead, having fallen from a horse onto the ground and having hit her head. We thought she would die. It was the worst seven hours of my life. Do you understand what that means, to be freshly married and to think your young bride is losing her life? It is a dark injustice. I have never felt anything like it.

PLURABELLE: We are so happy to see her well, eating dinner, radiant.

THE PRINCE FOR ALL SEASONS: It was your maid who nursed her back to health, and with such a sensitivity. My young bride took to her like a leaf to the sun. Isn't that right, darling?

THE YOUNG BRIDE: Yes.

THE PRINCE FOR ALL SEASONS: So you understand what I mean.

PLURABELLE: I do. It can only mean one thing: you want to take her from me.

THE PRINCE FOR ALL SEASONS: Yes, it is indeed that one thing. Exactly.

PLURABELLE: But she is almost my own daughter!

THE YOUNG BRIDE: Even my mother had to let me go, when I married the prince. Do you think she complains as you do now?

THE PRINCE FOR ALL SEASONS: She is very wise! Do you value your hotel?

PLURABELLE: I do!

THE PRINCE FOR ALL SEASONS: Then you shall keep it. And now you see the way the world goes. What one man wants, another must give up. Now we will all eat together. The magical Livinia is ours!

(*He holds up a platter.* THE YOUNG BRIDE *takes a drumstick, as does* LIVINIA.)

THE PRINCE FOR ALL SEASONS: (*smiling, to* THE YOUNG BRIDE) What was once impossible is now truly beautiful. I have you by my side, my dear, and there is not a star in the sky that does not weep from happiness.

(*He pulls his bride up and begins dancing with her, and forces the others to dance, too. The music slowly starts up as the lights begin to dim on the dancers.* MS. ODDI *has been playing ever more quietly, and no one has been paying attention. She is mortified.*)

Hotel hallway, late at night. MRS. SING *opens the door as* MS. ODDI, *with a travelling case in her hands, steps out of her hotel room, obviously in a great hurry. They run into each other.*

MRS. SING: Ms. Oddi!

MS. ODDI: Oh! Mrs. Sing! You startled me.

(MS. ODDI *turns, locks the door, then begins hurrying off.*)

MRS. SING: Are you leaving?

MS. ODDI: Oh, oh, I'm very sorry. Have they found Daniel?

MRS. SING: No, they have not.

MS. ODDI: Well, I'm very very sorry. I am sure they will find him tomorrow. I'm sure he will turn up. My daughter is convinced of it—

MRS. SING: You are very excited. You must catch your breath.

MS. ODDI: Oh, I have no time to catch my breath! I am in a great hurry!

(*She begins rustling in her purse.*)

MRS. SING: Where were you going?

MS. ODDI: Away. Just away.

MRS. SING: You are running away?

MS. ODDI: No, don't speculate!

MRS. SING: (*interrupting*) There is a great sadness in you. It is obvious to me, so perfectly obvious. You are like a wilting flower.

MS. ODDI: (*flustered*) Well, that's just life's way, isn't it?

MRS. SING: It doesn't have to be.

MS. ODDI: Of course it does!

MRS. SING: Life can be many ways. Come, think back on when you were little. How was life then?

MS. ODDI: No better than it is now, Mrs. Sing! No better! Please, move aside.

(*She makes to go.* MRS. SING *stops her.*)

MRS. SING: (*desperate*) Perhaps you have a secret you would like to share? That you could only share with another woman? There are so few of us here. We are both in families entirely of men.

MS. ODDI: That is not true! I have a daughter!

MRS. SING: But she is too young to count.

MS. ODDI: She certainly counts!

(MS. ODDI *hurries away.*)

MRS. SING: Ms. Oddi, you are making a great mistake! You could open up to me! We would tell each other all the little things in the world!

MS. ODDI: I owe you nothing! I owe you nothing!

JENNY *opens her eyes in her bed in her hotel room.* DAN *starts singing "A Million Votes for Jenny O" from the corner of the room. As the music continues,* JENNY *gets up and, drawn by the moonlight, goes and looks out the window at the moon hanging over Paris. She sighs—it's like her fantasy Paris, for the first time since she arrived. She is lit up with happiness. She watches the moon, smiling, hopeful.*

"A Million Votes for Jenny O"

Today before the storm
The angels made it known
That her house was the capital
That the sad, sad rain has been
A million votes for Jenny O
A million votes for Jenny O
A million votes for Jenny O
A million votes for Jenny O

(JENNY *pulls out a walkie-talkie from her pajama pocket and starts talking into it, again with such hope.*)

JENNY: Daniel… Daniel… if you can hear me, come in. Come in! We need you here, back at the hotel. If you are *anywhere* picking up this signal, please come in! Return to the hotel. Return to the hotel at once! Come in? Come in? This is Jenny O calling for Daniel Sing… come in, Daniel. Come in…

(JENNY *listens very carefully to the walkie-talkie, to see if she can pick up anything.*)

"A Million Votes for Jenny O" (cont'd)

I decided to make a fuss
Pitting her against Corey Elainus
On a sea of lies let's get lost
Like gifts to the storm
Like gifts to the storm
Da da da da da…

(*As the music gets more intense she hears voices from down below; she looks—it's* MR. ODDI *and* MS. ODDI *standing in the street, arguing with each other. She cannot hear what they're saying, though she strains to.*)

"A Million Votes for Jenny O" (cont'd)

Today before the storm
The angels made it known
That her house was the capital
That the sad, sad rain has been

A million votes for Jenny O

A million votes for Jenny O

A million votes for Jenny O

A million votes for Jenny O

(At the end of the song, MS. ODDI *runs off.* MR. ODDI *stands there alone, looking down at his hands, sadly. He turns to go back into the hotel, grasps the handle of the door, can't bring himself to enter, and sits down crumpled on the stoop. A cloud slowly moves over the moon.* JENNY *sits back on the edge of the bed, then curls into it and under the covers and lies there, eyes open wide.)*

ACT II

Cannes. MS. ODDI *and* MRS. SING *sit in wrought-iron chairs at a small, cafe-style table. It's the middle of the day. There may be greenery around. A little bill lies on the table, folded in two. Also, there are some items from* MS. ODDI's *purse—lipstick, tissue paper, a crossword-puzzle magazine. They drink from two tall glasses of soda.* MS. ODDI *is cold throughout the whole conversation.*

MRS. SING: I know it's something of an intrusion.

MS. ODDI: Well the traffic must have been very bad. The traffic getting in here is very bad.

MRS. SING: Yes, it was bad.

MS. ODDI: And where did you park your rental?

MRS. SING: By the hotel I am staying at.

MS. ODDI: My hotel?

MRS. SING: Yes.

(MS. ODDI *sips her drink. Nothing is said.*)

MS. ODDI: Have you been swimming yet?

MRS. SING: No, I just arrived at eleven o'clock. Then it took me a few hours to find you.

MS. ODDI: Do you think I have been suntanning?

MRS. SING: No.

MS. ODDI: I *have* been. With my friend!

MRS. SING: A woman?

MS. ODDI: A man. He put oil on my arms. See?

(*She holds out her arms.* MRS. SING *looks them over vaguely.*)

MRS. SING: Perhaps it's been absorbed into the skin.

(MS. ODDI *pulls her arms back.*)

MS. ODDI: Yes, well, you would say that. (*yawns*) The afternoons are so hot.

MRS. SING: (*eagerly*) You are greedy for more of the morning.

MS. ODDI: No I am not!

MRS. SING: I think I will go swimming this afternoon.

MS. ODDI: The sea is very blue.

MRS. SING: Have you been swimming?

MS. ODDI: Yes, I went for a swim this morning.

MRS. SING: If I go for a swim, where will you be this evening, when I return?

MS. ODDI: I suppose I'll be at the hotel, on the patio, reading my book.

MRS. SING: Then I'll go for a swim.

MS. ODDI: You shouldn't miss it while you're here.

MRS. SING: Yes...

MS. ODDI: And how long will you be here for?

MRS. SING: I don't know...

MS. ODDI: Have they found Daniel?

MRS. SING: No.

MS. ODDI: So perhaps you'll go back when they find him?

MRS. SING: Perhaps. I haven't thought it through. I didn't even bring a bikini.

MS. ODDI: You can buy so many on the boardwalk.

MRS. SING: Well then, that's what I'll do.

MS. ODDI: You'll buy yourself a bikini and take a swim. What'll you do about dinner?

MRS. SING: Perhaps you'd like to have dinner together?

MS. ODDI: No, thank you.

MRS. SING: You have plans?

MS. ODDI: Yes, I have plans! I have a friend. I have plans with him. He intends to take me to a lobster restaurant for dinner. *(annoyed)* Oh, I don't know why I'm telling you this.

MRS. SING: *(pleasantly, eagerly)* Perhaps you are becoming my friend.

(A WAITER comes out. MS. ODDI holds up the check.)

MS. ODDI: You charged us for an extra soda.

WAITER: Let's see.

(He looks at it. MS. ODDI watches him.)

WAITER: I don't know that this is an *extra* soda.

MS. ODDI: What do you mean? Clearly it's an extra soda. We only had one soda each.

WAITER: Well then, why does it say *soda* three times?

MS. ODDI: That's the mistake!

WAITER: *(talking slowly)* I don't normally make mistakes.

MRS. SING: That's why we call them mistakes! Look at our table. How many glasses do you see?

MS. ODDI: There's only two glasses. You're lying if you say there's a third.

WAITER: Well, I'll just take this back and fix it.

(He leaves.)

MS. ODDI: What a moron.

(*She begins packing up her purse with the articles lying on the table.*)

MRS. SING: Where are you going now?

MS. ODDI: I'm in a hurry.

MRS. SING: You're not going back to the hotel then, are you?

MS. ODDI: No, I'm seeing a two-thirty matinee. I have been seeing lots of movies. Movies every day!

MRS. SING: Don't you think it's bad to lose yourself in fantasy?

MS. ODDI: Never!

MRS. SING: Well, do what you like.

MS. ODDI: I'd appreciate it if you wouldn't worry about me. I can take care of myself well enough.

MRS. SING: Would you like my company?

MS. ODDI: No. Besides. I thought you needed a bikini.

MRS. SING: I do.

MS. ODDI: Then get your bikini!

(*The WAITER returns with the bill. MS. ODDI looks at it.*)

MS. ODDI: (*short*) Thank you.

WAITER: I took off the extra soda. It was my mistake.

MS. ODDI: I see that.

MRS. SING: Aren't you going to apologize to her now?

WAITER: I'm sorry.

MS. ODDI: It's not a problem.

MRS. SING: It was just a little headache.

(*The WAITER picks up their glasses.*)

MRS. SING: I'm not finished!

(*He puts it down, goes.*)

MRS. SING: (*to MS. ODDI*) They're so irresponsible. Show me one good waiter.

MS. ODDI: I haven't the time.

(*She gets up to rush off.*)

MRS. SING: Ms. Oddi!

MS. ODDI: Yes?

MRS. SING: I just wanted to tell you that you're looking very glamorous.

MS. ODDI: (*uncertain*) Well, thank you.

MRS. SING: It has done you good; the sea air, the escape.

MS. ODDI: I don't know what it's done me. Good-bye.

(She exits. MRS. SING stays at the table. The WAITER returns.)

MRS. SING: I am sorry for my friend's behavior.

WAITER: People come to this town for two nights, they think they own it. I'm used to it. It's the nature of a sea town. We're just ghosts to the people who come and stay in our hotels for two or three days. They don't believe this is home for anybody. Well, I make my memories here, too!

MRS. SING: We all make our memories here. We all make our memories wherever we go! I should report you to your manager.

(The WAITER walks off. MRS. SING looks around, begins to cry. She slaps the table, then takes out dark sunglasses from her purse and puts them on. She arranges her hair, licks her lips.)

MRS. SING: *(controlling tears)* What you need is a bikini... a bikini!

MS. ODDI's *hotel room.* MRS. SING *knocks on the door, letting herself in.*
MS. ODDI *is on her bed, doing her crossword puzzles. Through this whole*
conversation MS. ODDI *keeps her head down, focused on her magazine,*
filling in the crossword puzzle. She says her lines dutifully. MRS. SING *is*
eager, hanging about, nervous.

MRS. SING: Oh, Ms. Oddi, I'm terribly sorry. May I let myself in?

MS. ODDI: *(not looking up)* Fine.

MRS. SING: I hope you don't mind me bothering you. Have you eaten
already?

MS. ODDI: *(still not looking up)* I was going to eat at eight. I've always
liked eating late, but with Jenny, I never had the opportunity!

MRS. SING: Well, eight is very late. I've never understood how people
can eat so late. The stomach just gets hungry around six.

MS. ODDI: Did you take a swim?

MRS. SING: I took a swim, yes, thank you.

MS. ODDI: What color is it?

MRS. SING: What color is what? Oh! It's green. I prefer red as a color, but they didn't have a red bikini I particularly liked. I went to a few shops but at a certain point I said, Joy, just pick one. You're not going to be in a fashion show!

(*Pause.*)

MS. ODDI: I told you I am not interested in your friendship.

MRS. SING: If you could only see! If you would only give it a chance!

MS. ODDI: There's a very good reason I left Paris and my family behind. And it was not to start the same life all over again.

MRS. SING: What are you going to get in this new life?

MS. ODDI: I'm going to get everything I deserve.

MRS. SING: (*darkly*) Including a male friend?

MS. ODDI: (*looking up*) My new friend is the least of my concerns.

MRS. SING: You have a taste for new men?

MS. ODDI: (*looking back at her crossword*) Not at all.

(*There is a knocking at the door.*)

MS. ODDI: Come in.

(*THE MAN IN THE BEAR SUIT enters, wearing only his paws and feet.*)

THE MAN IN THE BEAR SUIT: Did I come at a bad time?

MS. ODDI: No.

THE MAN IN THE BEAR SUIT: Would you like to take a swim?

MS. ODDI: I would love one.

THE MAN IN THE BEAR SUIT: Let's go.

MS. ODDI: Just let me fill in this word.

(THE MAN IN THE BEAR SUIT *looks at* MRS. SING.)

THE MAN IN THE BEAR SUIT: Do you misbehave?

MRS. SING: *(indignant)* Never!

(He looks away.)

MS. ODDI: Ready.

THE MAN IN THE BEAR SUIT: Come along then.

(*She hops off the bed. They leave, closing the door behind them.* MRS. SING *flops herself down on the bed and begins to cry. She sits up.*)

MRS. SING: Don't cry, you fool. You are free. You are free!

(*She picks up the telephone, dials.*)

MRS. SING: Mrs. Lau? It is Mrs. Sing. Do you know where I am now? In Cannes!

THE MAN IN THE BEAR SUIT and MS. ODDI *sit on reclining patio chairs, after their swim, in towels. Perhaps* MS. ODDI *is without a top on.*

MS. ODDI: When my number comes up, I'm not going to miss it stuck with my family who doesn't appreciate me for anything. I gave my daughter a lot: discipline, self-respect, a sense of correctness.

THE MAN IN THE BEAR SUIT: Would you like a cigarette?

MS. ODDI: Yes. I haven't smoked since I was nineteen.

THE MAN IN THE BEAR SUIT: I'm sure you were very attractive when you were nineteen.

MS. ODDI: I whored myself around.

(*She takes a cigarette from him. He lights it.*)

MS. ODDI: Jenny is different. She is very prudish, very polite. Of course, she's barely thirteen. She has life in her, but… who knows?

THE MAN IN THE BEAR SUIT: It is so tedious to have a family.

(MRS. SING *enters.*)

MRS. SING: I thought I would find you here.

MS. ODDI: Have you eaten your dinner, Mrs. Sing?

MRS. SING: I ate my dinner, then I lay down.

MS. ODDI: Offer her a cigarette.

THE MAN IN THE BEAR SUIT: Would you like a cigarette?

MRS. SING: If I may.

(He hands her one. She puts it in her mouth. He goes to light it. She turns her face away.)

MRS. SING: No.

(She goes on "smoking" it.)

MRS. SING: I love the nightlife.

MS. ODDI: Mrs. Sing has come all the way from Cedervale. She is desperate to be my friend, and this is why you have been seeing her so often.

THE MAN IN THE BEAR SUIT: Why does she like you so much?

MS. ODDI: Because I am a woman.

THE MAN IN THE BEAR SUIT: Why do you like her so much?

MRS. SING: Please don't ask me any questions.

MS. ODDI: She has it in her mind that we could be friends. That we would tell each other everything; that we have so much in common.

MRS. SING: I'm not ashamed of it.

MS. ODDI: I have listened to this all day long. I listened to it while I was in Paris, too!

(THE MAN IN THE BEAR SUIT *leans over and starts squeezing* MS. ODDI's *breasts. She lets him, but doesn't respond.*)

MS. ODDI: Back in Paris, I had so much on my mind. It's incredible what happens to you when travelling. And then all of a sudden you stop, and you don't know where you are. It's terrifying to the death!

MRS. SING: You are absolutely right.

MS. ODDI: (*to* THE MAN IN THE BEAR SUIT) Come. If you are so eager we should go inside.

THE MAN IN THE BEAR SUIT: There is nobody here.

MS. ODDI: My back aches.

THE MAN IN THE BEAR SUIT: We'll go into the water.

MS. ODDI: We were just in the water! If I go in again I'll cramp up! Come along, we'll go back to my room. Or to your apartment. It's not so far.

THE MAN IN THE BEAR SUIT: (*upset*) It is not so far but it is full of people.

MS. ODDI: Then up to my room.

THE MAN IN THE BEAR SUIT: (*grumbling*) It is always full of miserable, freeloading people.

(*They go.*)

At a distance, JOHNNY ROCKETS *performs a free concert on the boardwalk.*
He is played by DAN—*but a minor costume change makes it clear it's an*
alternate version of DAN, DAN *at the height of a real or imagined, feared or*
fantasized about, fame. He sings.

"Johnny Rockets' Song"

It's gonna take an airplane

To get me off the ground

I don't blame anyone who isn't sticking around

Cause when you stick around

When you stick around

People like to put things in the ground

Now in my evil-empire eye

I'm going to be a star in the night sky above

So you think this is love

Yes I guess so, at least something to make it from

Dressed like a dream dreamt by *Lola* magazine

Baby you were born to be seen

And watch just the stars

Now step inside the widow-maker

Listen to your heart

Always the play never the thing

(MRS. SING and MS. ODDI appear on the beach. They are taking a long walk. They talk over the music, which is quieter now. They don't yet notice JOHNNY ROCKETS or the concert.)

MS. ODDI: Nobody has ever let me do what I wanted to. I always did what everyone *else* wanted me to do.

MRS. SING: That is a very stupid thing to say.

MS. ODDI: Nevertheless, it is true.

MRS. SING: Well, then you are on the verge of being mentally ill.

MS. ODDI: Still, when I think of myself at any age, I always think: what a precious thing you were. There was some way in which I was always trying to shield myself from every danger.

MRS. SING: Yes, you have already mentioned that!

(MS. ODDI sees JOHNNY ROCKETS.)

MS. ODDI: Oh no, it's Johnny Rockets.

MRS. SING: Who?

MS. ODDI: Jenny has his poster on her wall! Look how smooth he is. Knows just when to turn and everything.

MRS. SING: You shouldn't be so impressed. He's only a teenager. It comes naturally.

(She points to a HOBBLED MAN, who is also walking down the boardwalk. He carries a cage with a parakeet in it, maybe.)

MRS. SING: It takes more guts to be *that* man than your little Johnny Rockets.

(*JOHNNY ROCKETS begins signing autographs.*)

MS. ODDI: Come, let's go over.

(*She pulls MRS. SING by the hand toward JOHNNY ROCKETS and his crowd of adoring fans.*)

MS. ODDI: Johnny Rockets! Johnny Rockets!

(*Eventually JOHNNY ROCKETS looks over.*)

JOHNNY ROCKETS: Yes, mama?

MS. ODDI: (*calling*) How do you do it?

JOHNNY ROCKETS: Just like this, old lady!

(*He does a turn and swivels and flashes her a teen-idol grin. A roar of swoons goes up from the crowd.*)

JOHNNY ROCKETS: You like that, old lady?

MS. ODDI: (*giddy*) We're *big* fans!

(*JOHNNY ROCKETS pushes out of the crowd and comes toward MS. ODDI and MRS. SING.*)

JOHNNY ROCKETS: What are you two mamas doing on a day like today all alone on the boardwalk? Where are your husbands?

MRS. SING: (*priggish*) They're in Paris.

JOHNNY ROCKETS: You girls thought you'd take a joyride out to the sea? Take in a bit of sun, a bit of sand, some muscle on the beach? Hey, I could show you girls a real good time. You'd never have to tell your husbands about it. Come on, you're not too old for it, are you? You still get down, don't you?

MS. ODDI: *(coyly)* We were just taking a pleasant walk.

JOHNNY ROCKETS: Don't play that game, mama.

MS. ODDI: We were just talking a pleasant walk on such a nice day. Isn't it a nice day?

JOHNNY ROCKETS: Hell, every day's a nice day. Except for that man there! Probably every day's real shitty for that man there. Ain't that right, buddy?

THE HOBBLED MAN: What is?

JOHNNY ROCKETS: You got a good life or a shitty life?

MRS. SING: *(pulling MS. ODDI)* Come on, let's go.

MS. ODDI: *(resisting)* No, I'm curious.

MRS. SING: This will not be pleasant. We should not watch this interaction. It's sure to end in tears.

(MRS. SING pulls MS. ODDI off. JOHNNY ROCKETS pays attention to THE HOBBLED MAN.)

THE HOBBLED MAN: What can you do? I had some good years. That's all you can really ask for—two or three good years. Two or three good years is enough for a lifetime of happy memories! I'm not looking for adventures now. It's not so bad. When I was younger, I would do little dances when I was happy, like this—

(THE HOBBLED MAN *does a little dance.*)

THE HOBBLED MAN: But I never wanted anyone to see it. I was embarrassed about it. I never saw anyone else do these dances, so I was very ashamed! I hid myself. When people called me, I wouldn't go out in case I might forget myself and make a little dance of happiness. I didn't want anyone to laugh. Well, my friends started to notice that I would not go out when they called. They thought: He only ever invites us over when *he* feels like it. He never comes when we call him. It was true. I stayed at home, danced when I was happy, and never had anyone to be ashamed in front of. Soon all my friends drifted away. Then, over ten years, this hump developed. Can I say it is a bad life, as you put it? Well, no. I feed my animals with regularity, which I can't say I'd be able to do if I didn't have this isolation. Without this loneliness, I sure wouldn't have time for my animals. And it's something to have animals—*real* pets. I don't know if you've ever had a real pet?

(*During this speech,* JOHNNY ROCKETS's *demeanor has changed. He has become sad, humbled, uncool, brooding, lost his swagger. Some girls run up to him.*)

JOHNNY ROCKETS: Stop!

(JOHNNY ROCKETS *puts his hand out to stop them. He is mobbed.*)

MRS. SING, MS. ODDI, *and* THE MAN IN THE BEAR SUIT *at breakfast.* THE MAN IN THE BEAR SUIT *and* MS. ODDI *wear terry-cloth robes, while* MRS. SING *is more properly dressed. It's a continental breakfast.* MS. ODDI *is in a good mood;* MRS. SING *is not.*

MRS. SING: I didn't sleep a wink last night.

MS. ODDI: *(with a faint smile)* Perhaps you were enjoying yourself at last, Mrs. Sing.

MRS. SING: I am not an idiot and I know when I'm being made fun of.

THE MAN IN THE BEAR SUIT: Your friend didn't sleep a wink last night either. I was poking her all night.

MRS. SING: *(grumpy)* She is not my friend.

MS. ODDI: *(cheery)* Oh, Mrs. Sing. Don't say that. Of course you're my friend! Look at us here at breakfast.

MRS. SING: You told me I was not allowed to sit with you.

MS. ODDI: But here you are!

MRS. SING: That's right. I sat down anyway. There was no other table at which I could have felt more comfortable. But you put a little pot of jam on my seat while I was gone to get more coffee!

MS. ODDI: Don't be mad.

MRS. SING: If I'm mad I have a right to be! You have not treated me at all well since I arrived, not at all like a guest!

MS. ODDI: You're not a guest, you're an intruder! Where do you get off following me, simply because our children go to school together? You knew very well when I left Paris that I intended to be alone!

MRS. SING: I could tell you were in an irresponsible frame of mind.

MS. ODDI: That's a lie.

MRS. SING: If it's a lie it's a lie!

MS. ODDI: What a ludicrous thing to say. *(not mimicking, but explaining rather hysterically)* If it's a lie it's a lie and that was my point: it's a lie!

MRS. SING: If it's a lie, well, then, it's a lie!

THE MAN IN THE BEAR SUIT: You two are going in circles. Just going in circles.

(MS. ODDI stands up in a huff.)

MS. ODDI: *(sputtering)* I'm going back to my room. I did not leave Paris to carry on a routine!

(She exits.)

THE MAN IN THE BEAR SUIT: You are a terrible friend.

MRS. SING: It would look very different if she would pay some attention to me.

(MS. ODDI *returns*.)

MS. ODDI: There is so little one can do in life without someone looking over your shoulder, a person from the past! If there's anything to be learned from life, it's that a person looking over your shoulder all the time makes a woman too emotional! Too emotional! How are we supposed to *not* be emotional when someone's always waiting to see how we'll react! (*to* THE MAN IN THE BEAR SUIT) You're different of course, slightly, but if I knew you better, you'd be the same.

THE MAN IN THE BEAR SUIT: Moi?

MRS. SING: You're not a failure.

MS. ODDI: I'm not talking about failure!

(MS. ODDI *begins to cry*.)

THE MAN IN THE BEAR SUIT: Women always cry for themselves. You can be sure of one thing: when a woman is crying—it is for herself!

MS. ODDI: A man takes your body once and he thinks he owns you!

MRS. SING: That is right, Ms. Oddi, so you might as well go right back to your husband—to the man who *in fact* owns you. There's never an escape into other men.

MS. ODDI: (*red eyes*) Is that all you have to say?

MRS. SING: No... I would like to know if you would like to go swimming with me this afternoon.

MS. ODDI: This afternoon I shall be practicing my flute.

MRS. SING: And this evening?

MS. ODDI: This evening I will also practice my flute! Now I know that I did a true injustice to myself when I gave up the flute. That is where my talent lies, that is where my true worth always did lie, but I was too caught up in the world to know it!

MRS. SING: No one's true worth lies in a flute.

MS. ODDI: *(bitter, like a snake)* What do you know about the flute?

MRS. SING: Oh, please have tea with me, Ms. Oddi... there is so much we have to say to each other!

MS. ODDI: I will not! I cannot respond to every person in the world! People ask too much. It is impossible to find one's way in life when there's someone at every corner trying to manipulate your heart. How can I move forward in life if I am being tugged this way and that by everyone I meet? At a certain point a person must say Stop! No! I will live *my* life from now on. I will think *my* thoughts. I will dream *my* dreams. *(hysterical)* Why should I feel guilty about it? I have spent my entire life feeling what everyone else feels! And do you know what makes a woman lose her youth? Sympathy! Too much sympathy! Certainly there are feelings everywhere; must we respond to each one of them?

THE MAN IN THE BEAR SUIT: See how she talks? She goes on and on, like a little toy.

(*Delighted by her presumption, he starts to fondle her.*)

MRS. SING: And yet Ms. Oddi—your sympathy would make me feel so much better.

MS. ODDI: My first boyfriend—oh, he smoked a very big pipe—he always said: Men make the world, and women decorate it. Well, it turns out he was right! That is all I have done—decorated! Decorated my family with my presence…

(*She begins to cry again.*)

THE MAN IN THE BEAR SUIT: (*slaps her*) Stop that.

(*She stops crying.*)

MRS. SING: Well, Ms. Oddi. There is certainly no other woman like you in the world!

MS. ODDI: Yes, I have often been told.

(MRS. SING *starts to cry.*)

MS. ODDI: (*scornful*) Now what are you crying for?

MRS. SING: (*crying*) But what about love, Ms. Oddi? The heart is our only guide. If you turn off your heart, you will be absolutely spinning in circles!

MS. ODDI: You are wrong, Mrs. Sing. It is the heart which makes us spin in circles! The heart!

THE MAN IN THE BEAR SUIT: Come along—no more talking. You give me a headache with all your little words!

(*He drags* MS. ODDI *off by the arm.*)

MRS. SING: (*calling*) What about the ocean?

MS. ODDI: (*calling back*) What do you take me for? A submarine? I don't want the ocean. I am an airplane, Mrs. Sing! (*finger pointed at the sky, arm raised*) I spend my time in the air!

MRS. SING *wanders into the hotel lobby, where there is a small store. She lifts a bikini off a hanger and holds it in front of her body, turning this way and that in front of the mirror. She feels tremendously lonely.* DAN *is nearby, singing "Submarines Don't Mind."*

"Submarines Don't Mind"

Submarines don't mind
Spending their time in the ocean
Spending their time in the ocean
(repeat and repeat…)

(As she moves back and forth in front of the mirror, she begins to feel even worse. She puts the bikini back on the hanger, then goes to the hotel phone, begins dialing, then puts down the phone slowly. She looks around the lobby, then hurries into an elevator, having made up her mind.)

Hallway of the hotel in Cannes. MRS. SING, *dressed to travel and carrying a suitcase, is heading down the hall. The music from the previous scene continues.* MS. ODDI, *a little drunk, in a beautiful gown, steps out into the hall and hurries after* MRS SING.

MS. ODDI: Oh! Where are you going?

MRS. SING: *(escaping)* Good-bye, Ms. Oddi.

MS. ODDI: Good-bye? *(clearly drunk)* What do you mean, *good-bye?*

MRS. SING: I am returning to Paris.

MS. ODDI: But… we're only just becoming friends! Don't you want to stay and be my *friend?*

MRS. SING: Oh, Ms. Oddi. I am such a fool. You don't want to be my friend.

MS. ODDI: But Mrs. Sing—where did you get that idea? You are so sensitive! You know I was just pretending! *(flamboyantly, drunk)* I was just joking around…

MRS. SING: No, I'm not like you, Ms. Oddi. I have to go home now.

MS. ODDI: Not like *me?* But what am I like?

*(*MRS. SING *begins to head off.)*

MS. ODDI: Well I—(*haughty, defensive, suddenly sober*) All I wanted is a better life!

(MRS. SING *pauses, turns.*)

MRS. SING: There *is* no better life, Ms. Oddi. There is no better life.

(MRS. SING *leaves.*)

THE MAN IN THE BEAR SUIT sits in the hotel bar while DAN sings "An Actor's Revenge." THE MAN IN THE BEAR SUIT drinks. His costume is half-off, as though he's tired of pretending. MS. ODDI enters and begins to drink at the other end of the bar. Seeing THE MAN IN THE BEAR SUIT, she moves over to him. He takes a look at her, then turns purposefully away. Another woman comes in, and he is happy to see her and drinks with her. There are no words in this scene, just DAN singing.

"An Actor's Revenge"

An actor will seek revenge
I don't know why and I don't know when
There'll be talk, there'll be action
Demanding satisfaction
Girls, oh you hate to play a girl
An actor will seek revenge
He came on too strong
He was weird, he was wrong
A bloodless commandant throwing everybody out
The kids twist and shout
Until the world fucking wrecks it
A boulevardier might say
Tomorrow's another day

All right, yes, but it's also just another mess

Crime and punishment, no that's not what I meant

An actor will seek revenge

I don't know why and I don't know when

There'll be talk, there'll be action

Demanding satisfaction

Girls, oh you hate to be a girl

An actor will seek revenge

Upon the one who vetted those ridiculous lines

Saying what we really need now is an emotional history

Of the Lower East Side

Cause it was wild, it was wild,

Oh no, here we go again

MS. ODDI *sits on the bed of her hotel room. She picks up her flute—wants to play it—puts it to her lips—tries a bit—but is horrible. She stops and puts it down, lost. She sits there for a bit, not knowing what to do. She picks up the phone, pushes one number, listens.*

MS. ODDI: Room 313.

(There is a knock on her door. She opens it. The HOTELIER *stands there before her.)*

MS. ODDI: How does one get to Jamaica from Cannes?

HOTELIER: A bus comes every half hour for the airport. *(points to the ceiling)* Then you're in the sky.

A bus that says AIRPORT *across the front carries along* MS. ODDI *and* THE HANDSOME MAN. *They are not sitting together. The music continues.*

In front of the Paris hotel. MR. SING *stands at its entrance.* MRS. SING *comes up the walk with her suitcase.*

MRS. SING: I'm sorry.

MR. SING: You have shamed me and you have shamed your son, and you have shamed yourself!

MRS. SING: Did they find him?

MR. SING: No.

(They look at each other. MRS. SING *wants to go into the hotel—tries to push past her husband—but he won't let her through.)*

MRS. SING: Please let me in. I am very tired.

MR. SING: You cannot go inside!

MRS. SING: Why not?

MR. SING: Because I have told them not to let you in here! How am I to consider you a wife? No, you go and find the hotel that accepts such wives. This hotel would never!

*(*MRS. SING *tries to touch him; he pushes her away.)*

MR. SING: I was going to give you a good shake! I can give it to you anyways!

(*He gives her a rough shake.*)

MR. SING: (*while shaking her, frustrated*) This is the least of my concerns, shaking you!

(MRS. SING *notices something in the distance.*)

MRS. SING: I think it's Daniel!

MR. SING: Where? Daniel!

(*They watch as two* CONSTABLES *come in, holding* DANIEL *between them.* DANIEL *is handcuffed. They uncuff him, shove him.*)

MRS. SING: Daniel!

CONSTABLE 1: Tell your parents where you've been.

DANIEL: No.

MR. SING: Tell us, Daniel!

DANIEL: No.

CONSTABLE 2: We found him in the gutter!

MRS. SING: (*aghast*) The gutter!

DANIEL: In fact, I was standing on a corner.

MR. SING: Don't talk back!

CONSTABLE 2: Going to disrespect your mother, eh?

(CONSTABLE 2 *slugs him.*)

MR. SING: We have been sick! Where did you go!

CONSTABLE 2: Are you going to tell your father where you were?

DANIEL: No.

(CONSTABLE 2 *punches him in the stomach.*)

MRS. SING: Who were you were with!

CONSTABLE 2: Are you going to tell them who you were with, you little maggot?

(CONSTABLE 2 *shoves him to the ground and stands over him, then kicks him.*)

CONSTABLE 2: You shit.

MRS. SING: Where were you!

(CONSTABLE 2 *kicks him again.*)

CONSTABLE 2: The shit.

MR. SING: He ran away.

CONSTABLE 1: He's yours again. Should we leave him?

MR. SING: Yes, do.

(CONSTABLE *1 kicks* DANIEL *in the side.* CONSTABLE *2 turns and spits on him. They exit.* MR. SING *grabs* MRS. SING's *arm and they go into the hotel.* DANIEL *lies there. He picks a cigarette from inside his jacket and lights it, then smokes it.*)

DANIEL: I went to a whorehouse... I walked along the Seine. Of course they didn't let me sleep with any of the ladies. I had no money. Still, I thought, there's a lot I can do without any money. I know my worth. I'm handsome. Stranger things have happened than a thirteen-year-old boy getting by on his own. This is what life is all about, I thought—survival, what they mean by survival. I could have gone on forever, could have lived like that forever. Everything I needed... I found it. It was perfect. You don't truly feel alive until you're a grown-up, until you really have to survive. Until you're a grown-up, you have no idea what life is. But man, I know it now. You can't rest for a second. You can't let yourself go for a moment. Like a soldier—like a wild animal. Everything matters. You slip up, you're dead. Step off the wrong curb, you're dead. Being a grown-up is great. Tense, like a fighter. None of this fooling around. All of it matters. Everything you do is important; it's life or death. None of this bullshit playing around, kid stuff. Pure adrenalin, being a grown-up. You look the wrong way, you die. No one's going to tell you which way to look. It's up to you. All in your hands. Yeah, they've got it, grown-ups, the secret of life. They're holding it all in their hands. And it's great, the world. I love it. It's great.

(*DANIEL begins to sing this song, or maybe* DAN *does, or both, or one then the other. It is clear now, once and for all, that* DANIEL *and* DAN *are the same person.*)

"Daniel's Song"

I thought I was on the inside
But now I know it's all a secret
The three of us together forever in debt
I sat down and took a number
At the table where death resides
Borrowed an ascot to cover my eyes
From the fame that awaited
Now these beautiful days just seem dated…

(*The guitar strumming continues over the next scene.*)

JENNY *and* DANIEL *sit on the steps of the hotel. It is early evening.* JENNY'S *bags are beside her.* PLURABELLE, *in rattier clothes, moves past them, sweeping.* DANIEL *tries to be attentive. He has a more grown-up air.* JENNY *seems young by comparison. There's something stunted about her now, stupid, hysterical, trying to cover up everything inside.*

JENNY: We're going home soon.

DANIEL: Good. Good for you.

JENNY: We couldn't find her but my dad said she'd come back. I thought we were going to stay in Paris until we found her but my dad said we should just go home and that she'd know to find us there.

DANIEL: Why not?

JENNY: It makes sense. She knows that's our home much better than she knows that this is our home. This is not our home, this is just the hotel we were staying in.

DANIEL: Sure, it was a vacation.

JENNY: Yes, just where we were staying on our vacation. It's not our home like back home is, where our school is. This is not our home the way that that is our home.

DANIEL: *(tired of this)* Yes Jenny, I understand. Your home is in Cedervale, not here in Paris.

JENNY: Right, and same with my mother.

DANIEL: And same with your father.

JENNY: That's all I was saying. Whatever. I don't care. It's not like I care.

(She takes out a balloon and tries to blow it up. Laughs nervously. It won't inflate.)

JENNY: Oh shit. Oh shit. It's not working.

DANIEL: Here, let me.

JENNY: No, no. No, no.

(She begins blowing it up again, unsuccessful as before.)

JENNY: I have to do it myself. *(continues blowing it)* I can do it.

(It doesn't work.)

JENNY: Oh shoot. Oh well.

(She puts it in her pocket.)

JENNY: *(a little hysterical)* I suppose I'll try later. I'm sick of this hotel anyway. I miss so much about back home. For instance, the baseball diamond. Hello, who the hell would have thought I loved that shitty baseball diamond? But it made a big impact on me. A great impact.

I realize now I'm a fan of baseball diamonds. I'll do whatever I can, in this new life, to enjoy myself at the baseball diamonds.

DANIEL: What do you mean, "this new life"?

JENNY: Oh shit Daniel, you get what I mean. We have an understanding. I knew all along you'd be back. I was counting on it. I figured you wandered off in the parade. You must have seen some girl you liked.

DANIEL: No, I didn't.

JENNY: You must really have liked her, boy, to have sure scared the shit out of your parents! I was convinced we were going to find you though, Daniel. It was even my idea to look for you in the park. You weren't hiding in the park, Daniel, were you?

DANIEL: No.

JENNY: I wouldn't talk to you about girl stuff if I didn't think you'd understand—

DANIEL: Don't, Jenny. Please don't.

JENNY: It's about my period—

DANIEL: Don't.

(*JENNY falls silent. Looks at her toes.*)

DANIEL: I'm going inside now, Jenny. I'm sorry.

(*He goes inside.*)

MR. ODDI and JENNY *walk slowly across the stage holding hands, carrying their suitcases. It is early evening. They are on their way home. Their airplane tickets stick out of the pocket of* MR. ODDI's *suit jacket.* DAN *sings, but we don't see him—it's the first time we don't see him when he's singing.*

"Daniel's Song" *(cont'd)*

Da da da da da da da da da da...

The lights come up on this scene suddenly. Jamaica. DANIEL *lounges on a beach chair. He is strumming the "Daniel's Song" melody, mostly to himself, using* DAN's *guitar. An older* JENNY—*in her twenties or thirties, the same age* DAN *has been all along—comes in, wearing sunglasses and a glamorous wrap. She is smiling happily. She sits beside* DANIEL, *who begins to sing.*

"Daniel's Song" *(repeat)*

> I thought I was on the inside
> But now I know it's all a secret
> The three of us together forever in debt
> I sat down and took a number
> At the table where death resides
> Borrowed an ascot to cover my eyes
> From the fame that awaited
> Now these beautiful days just seem dated...

JENNY: *(interrupting him; he stops playing)* Oh, Daniel, that was so long ago. Who cares anymore? It's nothing. It's over.

*(*DANIEL *and* JENNY *smile at each other and kiss.* JENNY *takes off her robe. She goes into the ocean and swims around.* DANIEL *stands to watch her.*)*

DANIEL: I care. I've written something for you, Jenny.

(He serenades her with this gentle, heartfelt song, which he sings with more conviction than any of the previous songs. At some point, while he plays, the curtain comes down behind him.)

"Don't Become The Thing You Hated"

Don't become

Don't become

Don't become the thing you hated

The thing you hated

The thing you hated *(verse repeats)*

Suns rise and sun go down again

Open your Strathcona doors

Let him in, let him in, let him in, let him in *(repeat)*

Don't become

Don't become

Don't become the thing you hated

The thing you hated

The thing you hated

The thing you hated

(When the song is done, there is canned cheering, canned applause. He bows, then turns and pushes himself through the curtain.)

THE END

About the artists

Sheila Heti is the author of six books, including the children's book *We Need a Horse* and the story collection *The Middle Stories*. She lives in Toronto.

Dan Bejar is a singer-songwriter, best known for his work with The New Pornographers, and for his band, Destroyer. He lives in Vancouver.

Thank You

Kelly Thornton and Toronto's Nightwood Theatre, for commissioning the play; Erica Kopyto; the early workshop directors, Benuta Rubes and Chris Abraham; all the actors who participated in the workshops, in particular Kathleen Phillips, who played a memorable Jenny Oddi; Dan Bejar for the excellent songs; for love and encouragement, Lucas Rebick, Margaux Williamson, Misha Glouberman, Carl Wilson, and Jacob Richmond; all those who participated in the backyard reading, including Jon Davies, Sholom Glouberman, Sholem Krishtalka, Amy Lam, Nika Mistruzzi, Sean O'Neill, Liz Peterson, and Alvin Rebick; Marc Bendavid for the backyard; Lena Dunham; Marie-Helene Westgate; Andrew Leland and McSweeney's for being so game; Melissa Srbinovich, for her wise counsel on bringing the play to New York; Warby Parker for their generous funding of the production; everyone who contributed to our Indiegogo campaign; Harbourfront Festival's World Stage; the wonderful and wonderfully fun cast of *All Our Happy Days Are Stupid*; the show's talented and tireless creative team, in particular Erin Brubacher and Zack Russell; Videofag's William Ellis; the original Toronto audience; the excellent staff of The Kitchen, especially Lumi Tan; and finally deepest gratitude to Jordan Bass and Jordan Tannahill, for taking something that might not have been and turning it into something that was.